This Maid of Honor Planner Belongs To

____

____

Hey! Thanks for purchasing this book and hope it helps you on your journey. All feedback on Amazon is appreciated. We have put a lot of effort into this title, so if you are not completely satisfied email thechikkupublishing@gmail.com. You're **INVITED** to receive a **Digital copy of 2021 Planner** at https://www.chikkupublishing.com

Save The Important Dates

Wedding Date On: _______________________

Mailing By: _______________________

Coordinate Gift Registry By: _______________________

Dress Shopping On: _______________________

Meet Caterer On: _______________________

Invitations Mail By: _______________________

Bridal Shower On: _______________________

Final Dress Alteration On: _______________________

Final Guest List By: _______________________

Bridal Party On: _______________________

Prep. On Hair & Nails: _______________________

12 Months Planner

January 2021

Sun	Mon	Tue	Wed	Thu	Fri	Sat
27	28	29	30	31	1	2
3	4	5	6	7	8	9
10	11	12	13	14	15	16
17	18	19	20	21	22	23
24	25	26	27	28	29	30
31	1	2	3	4	5	6

Monthly Planner

February 2021

Sun	Mon	Tue	Wed	Thu	Fri	Sat
31	1	2	3	4	5	6
7	8	9	10	11	12	13
14	15	16	17	18	19	20
21	22	23	24	25	26	27
28	1	2	3	4	5	6

Monthly Planner

March 2021

Sun	Mon	Tue	Wed	Thu	Fri	Sat
28	1	2	3	4	5	6
7	8	9	10	11	12	13
14	15	16	17	18	19	20
21	22	23	24	25	26	27
28	29	30	31	1	2	3

____

____

____

April 2021

Sun	Mon	Tue	Wed	Thu	Fri	Sat
28	29	30	31	1	2	3
4	5	6	7	8	9	10
11	12	13	14	15	16	17
18	19	20	21	22	23	24
25	26	27	28	29	30	1

Monthly Planner

May 2021

Sun	Mon	Tue	Wed	Thu	Fri	Sat
25	26	27	28	29	30	1
2	3	4	5	6	7	8
9	10	11	12	13	14	15
16	17	18	19	20	21	22
23	24	25	26	27	28	29
30	31	1	2	3	4	5

Monthly Planner

June 2021

Sun	Mon	Tue	Wed	Thu	Fri	Sat
30	31	1	2	3	4	5
6	7	8	9	10	11	12
13	14	15	16	17	18	19
20	21	22	23	24	25	26
27	28	29	30	1	2	3

Monthly Planner

July 2021

Sun	Mon	Tue	Wed	Thu	Fri	Sat
27	28	29	30	1	2	3
4	5	6	7	8	9	10
11	12	13	14	15	16	17
18	19	20	21	22	23	24
25	26	27	28	29	30	31

____

____

____

Monthly Planner

August 2021

Sun	Mon	Tue	Wed	Thu	Fri	Sat
1	2	3	4	5	6	7
8	9	10	11	12	13	14
15	16	17	18	19	20	21
22	23	24	25	26	27	28
29	30	31	1	2	3	4

____

____

____

Monthly Planner

September 2021

Sun	Mon	Tue	Wed	Thu	Fri	Sat
29	30	31	1	2	3	4
5	6	7	8	9	10	11
12	13	14	15	16	17	18
19	20	21	22	23	24	25
26	27	28	29	30	1	2

Monthly Planner

October 2021

Sun	Mon	Tue	Wed	Thu	Fri	Sat
26	27	28	29	30	1	2
3	4	5	6	7	8	9
10	11	12	13	14	15	16
17	18	19	20	21	22	23
24	25	26	27	28	29	30
31	1	2	3	4	5	6

Monthly Planner

November 2021

Sun	Mon	Tue	Wed	Thu	Fri	Sat
31	1	2	3	4	5	6
7	8	9	10	11	12	13
14	15	16	17	18	19	20
21	22	23	24	25	26	27
28	29	30	1	2	3	4

Monthly Planner

December 2021

Sun	Mon	Tue	Wed	Thu	Fri	Sat
28	29	30	1	2	3	4
5	6	7	8	9	10	11
12	13	14	15	16	17	18
19	20	21	22	23	24	25
26	27	28	29	30	31	1

2 Weeks Planner Before Wedding Day (By Day)

IMPORTANT

SCHEDULE

6AM

8AM

10AM

12PM

2PM

3PM

4PM

5PM

6PM

7PM

8PM

9PM

SUNDAY

TODAY'S TASKS

MONDAY

IMPORTANT

SCHEDULE

6AM

8AM

10AM

12PM

2PM

3PM

4PM

5PM

6PM

7PM

8PM

9PM

TODAY'S TASKS

TUESDAY

IMPORTANT

SCHEDULE

6AM

8AM

10AM

12PM

2PM

3PM

4PM

5PM

6PM

7PM

8PM

9PM

TODAY'S TASKS

IMPORTANT

SCHEDULE

6AM

8AM

10AM

12PM

2PM

3PM

4PM

5PM

6PM

7PM

8PM

9PM

WEDNESDAY

TODAY'S TASKS

THURSDAY

IMPORTANT

SCHEDULE

6AM

8AM

10AM

12PM

2PM

3PM

4PM

5PM

6PM

7PM

8PM

9PM

TODAY'S TASKS

IMPORTANT

SCHEDULE

6AM

8AM

10AM

12PM

2PM

3PM

4PM

5PM

6PM

7PM

8PM

9PM

FRIDAY

TODAY'S TASKS

IMPORTANT

SCHEDULE

6AM

8AM

10AM

12PM

2PM

3PM

4PM

5PM

6PM

7PM

8PM

9PM

SATURDAY

TODAY'S TASKS

IMPORTANT

SCHEDULE

6AM

8AM

10AM

12PM

2PM

3PM

4PM

5PM

6PM

7PM

8PM

9PM

SUNDAY

TODAY'S TASKS

MONDAY

IMPORTANT

SCHEDULE

6AM

8AM

10AM

12PM

2PM

3PM

4PM

5PM

6PM

7PM

8PM

9PM

TODAY'S TASKS

Weekly Planner (2nd Wk)

IMPORTANT

TUESDAY

SCHEDULE

6AM

8AM

10AM

12PM

2PM

3PM

4PM

5PM

6PM

7PM

8PM

9PM

TODAY'S TASKS

Weekly Planner (1ˢᵗ Wk)

IMPORTANT

SCHEDULE

6AM

8AM

10AM

12PM

2PM

3PM

4PM

5PM

6PM

7PM

8PM

9PM

WEDNESDAY

TODAY'S TASKS

THURSDAY

IMPORTANT

SCHEDULE

6AM

8AM

10AM

12PM

2PM

3PM

4PM

5PM

6PM

7PM

8PM

9PM

TODAY'S TASKS

Weekly Planner (1st Wk)

FRIDAY

IMPORTANT

SCHEDULE

6AM

8AM

10AM

12PM

2PM

3PM

4PM

5PM

6PM

7PM

8PM

9PM

TODAY'S TASKS

SATURDAY

IMPORTANT

SCHEDULE

6AM

8AM

10AM

12PM

2PM

3PM

4PM

5PM

6PM

7PM

8PM

9PM

TODAY'S TASKS

Bridal Party Contact List

Bridal Party Contact List

Name: ____

Address: ____

Phone Number: ____

E-mail Address: ____

Gift: ____

Save The Day Card Sent	♡	Invitation Sent	♡	R.S.V.P Received	♡	Thank you Sent	♡	Number Attending

---

Name: ____

Address: ____

Phone Number: ____

E-mail Address: ____

Gift: ____

Save The Day Card Sent	♡	Invitation Sent	♡	R.S.V.P Received	♡	Thank you Sent	♡	Number Attending

---

Name: ____

Address: ____

Phone Number: ____

E-mail Address: ____

Gift: ____

Save The Day Card Sent	♡	Invitation Sent	♡	R.S.V.P Received	♡	Thank you Sent	♡	Number Attending

Bridal Party Contact List

Name: ____

Address: ____

Phone Number: ____

E-mail Address: _______________________________________

Gift: ____

Save The Day Card Sent	♥	Invitation Sent	♥	R. S. V. P. Received	♥	Thank you Sent	♥	Number Attending
		_______	_______	_______	_______	_______		

Name: ____

Address: ____

Phone Number: ____

E-mail Address: _______________________________________

Gift: ____

Save The Day Card Sent	♥	Invitation Sent	♥	R. S. V. P. Received	♥	Thank you Sent	♥	Number Attending
		_______	_______	_______	_______	_______		

Name: ____

Address: ____

Phone Number: ____

E-mail Address: _______________________________________

Gift: ____

Save The Day Card Sent	♥	Invitation Sent	♥	R. S. V. P. Received	♥	Thank you Sent	♥	Number Attending
		_______	_______	_______	_______	_______		

Bridal Party Contact List

Name: _______________________________________

Address: _______________________________________

Phone Number: _______________________________________

E-mail Address: _______________________________________

Gift: _______________________________________

Save The Day Card Sent ♡ Invitation Sent ♡ R.S.V.P. Received ♡ Thank you Sent ♡ Number Attending
_______ _______ _______ _______ _______

Name: _______________________________________

Address: _______________________________________

Phone Number: _______________________________________

E-mail Address: _______________________________________

Gift: _______________________________________

Save The Day Card Sent ♡ Invitation Sent ♡ R.S.V.P. Received ♡ Thank you Sent ♡ Number Attending
_______ _______ _______ _______ _______

Name: _______________________________________

Address: _______________________________________

Phone Number: _______________________________________

E-mail Address: _______________________________________

Gift: _______________________________________

Save The Day Card Sent ♡ Invitation Sent ♡ R.S.V.P. Received ♡ Thank you Sent ♡ Number Attending
_______ _______ _______ _______ _______

Bridal Party Contact List

Name: _______________________________________

Address: _______________________________________

Phone Number: _______________________________________

E-mail Address: _______________________________________

Gift: _______________________________________

Save The Day Card Sent	♥	Invitation Sent	♥	R.S.V.P Received	♥	Thank you Sent	♥	Number Attending
								_______

Name: _______________________________________

Address: _______________________________________

Phone Number: _______________________________________

E-mail Address: _______________________________________

Gift: _______________________________________

Save The Day Card Sent	♥	Invitation Sent	♥	R.S.V.P Received	♥	Thank you Sent	♥	Number Attending
								_______

Name: _______________________________________

Address: _______________________________________

Phone Number: _______________________________________

E-mail Address: _______________________________________

Gift: _______________________________________

Save The Day Card Sent	♥	Invitation Sent	♥	R.S.V.P Received	♥	Thank you Sent	♥	Number Attending
								_______

Bridal Party Contact List

Name: ____

Address: ____

Phone Number: ____________________________________

E-mail Address: ___________________________________

Gift: ____

Save The Day Card Sent	♡	Invitation Sent	♡	R.S.V.P. Received	♡	Thank you Sent	♡	Number Attending

Name: ____

Address: ____

Phone Number: ____________________________________

E-mail Address: ___________________________________

Gift: ____

Save The Day Card Sent	♡	Invitation Sent	♡	R.S.V.P. Received	♡	Thank you Sent	♡	Number Attending

Name: ____

Address: ____

Phone Number: ____________________________________

E-mail Address: ___________________________________

Gift: ____

Save The Day Card Sent	♡	Invitation Sent	♡	R.S.V.P. Received	♡	Thank you Sent	♡	Number Attending

Bridal Shower Party

Bridal Party Planner

LOCATION: BUDGET:

TIME: DATE: NUMBER OF GUESTS:

PARTY BUDGET

ITEMS	BUDGET	ACTUAL AMOUNT
TOTAL		

THINGS TO BUY

DECORS	GROCERIES

SCHEDULE

TO - DOS

- ☐
- ☐
- ☐
- ☐
- ☐
- ☐
- ☐
- ☐
- ☐
- ☐

Bridal Party Planner

LOCATION: **BUDGET:**

TIME: **DATE:**   **NUMBER OF GUESTS:**

PARTY BUDGET

ITEMS	BUDGET	ACTUAL AMOUNT
TOTAL		

THINGS TO BUY

DECORS	GROCERIES

SCHEDULE

TO - DOS

- [ ]
- [ ]
- [ ]
- [ ]
- [ ]
- [ ]
- [ ]
- [ ]
- [ ]
- [ ]

Bridal Party Planner

LOCATION:

BUDGET:

TIME:

DATE:

NUMBER OF GUESTS:

PARTY BUDGET

ITEMS	BUDGET	ACTUAL AMOUNT
TOTAL		

THINGS TO BUY

DECORS	GROCERIES

SCHEDULE

TO - DOS

- [ ]
- [ ]
- [ ]
- [ ]
- [ ]
- [ ]
- [ ]
- [ ]
- [ ]
- [ ]

Bridal Party Planner

LOCATION:		BUDGET:

TIME:	DATE:	NUMBER OF GUESTS:

PARTY BUDGET

ITEMS	BUDGET	ACTUAL AMOUNT
TOTAL		

THINGS TO BUY

DECORS	GROCERIES

SCHEDULE

TO - DOS

- [ ]
- [ ]
- [ ]
- [ ]
- [ ]
- [ ]
- [ ]
- [ ]
- [ ]
- [ ]
- [ ]

Bridal Party Planner

LOCATION:

BUDGET:

TIME:

DATE:

NUMBER OF GUESTS:

PARTY BUDGET

ITEMS	BUDGET	ACTUAL AMOUNT
TOTAL		

THINGS TO BUY

DECORS	GROCERIES

SCHEDULE

TO - DOS

- [ ]
- [ ]
- [ ]
- [ ]
- [ ]
- [ ]
- [ ]
- [ ]
- [ ]
- [ ]

Bridal Shower Games and Activities

♡

- Love Songs
- Doubles Jenga
- Bride and Groom Photo Challenge
- Bingo Gift Game
- Wedding Ring Toss
- Romantic Movie Quotes
- Ball and Chain Game
- Bride and Groom Trivia
- Favourite Dates Activity
- Wedding Catch Phrase

Bridal Shower
Games and Activities

♡

Bridal Shower
Games and Activities

♡

- [ ]
- [ ]
- [ ]
- [ ]
- [ ]
- [ ]
- [ ]
- [ ]
- [ ]
- [ ]
- [ ]
- [ ]

Bridal Shower
Games and Activities

♡

- [ ]
- [ ]
- [ ]
- [ ]
- [ ]
- [ ]
- [ ]
- [ ]
- [ ]
- [ ]
- [ ]
- [ ]

Bridal Shower
Games and Activities

♡

- [ ]
- [ ]
- [ ]
- [ ]
- [ ]
- [ ]
- [ ]
- [ ]
- [ ]
- [ ]
- [ ]
- [ ]

Bridal Shower
Games and Activities

♡

- [ ]
- [ ]
- [ ]
- [ ]
- [ ]
- [ ]
- [ ]
- [ ]
- [ ]
- [ ]
- [ ]
- [ ]

Bridal Shower
Games and Activities

♡

- [ ]
- [ ]
- [ ]
- [ ]
- [ ]
- [ ]
- [ ]
- [ ]
- [ ]
- [ ]
- [ ]

Bridal Shower
Games and Activities

♡

- [ ]
- [ ]
- [ ]
- [ ]
- [ ]
- [ ]
- [ ]
- [ ]
- [ ]
- [ ]
- [ ]
- [ ]

Bridal Shower
Games and Activities

♡

- [ ]
- [ ]
- [ ]
- [ ]
- [ ]
- [ ]
- [ ]
- [ ]
- [ ]
- [ ]
- [ ]
- [ ]

Bridal Shower
Games and Activities
♡

- [ ] ____
- [ ] ____
- [ ] ____
- [ ] ____
- [ ] ____
- [ ] ____
- [ ] ____
- [ ] ____
- [ ] ____
- [ ] ____
- [ ] ____
- [ ] ____

Bridal Shower
Games and Activities
♡

The Wedding Day

Wedding To-Do List Day

Wedding To-Do List Day

Wedding To-Do List Day

Wedding To-Do List Day

- [ ]
- [ ]
- [ ]
- [ ]
- [ ]
- [ ]
- [ ]
- [ ]
- [ ]
- [ ]
- [ ]

Wedding To-Do List Day

Wedding Actual Day

ACTIVITES		ROLES

NOTES

Wedding Actual Day

ACTIVITES		ROLES

NOTES

Wedding Actual Day

ACTIVITES		ROLES

NOTES

Wedding Actual Day

ACTIVITES		ROLES

NOTES

Wedding Actual Day

ACTIVITES	

ROLES

NOTES

Special Notes & Ideas

Special Notes & Ideas

Special Notes & Ideas

Special Notes & Ideas

Special Notes & Ideas

Special Notes & Ideas

Special Notes & Ideas

Special Notes & Ideas

Special Notes & Ideas

Special Notes & Ideas

Wedding Memories & Photographs

Wedding Memories & Photographs

Wedding Memories & Photographs

Wedding Memories & Photographs

Wedding Memories & Photographs

Wedding Memories & Photographs

Wedding Memories & Photographs

Wedding Memories & Photographs

Wedding Memories & Photographs

Wedding Memories & Photographs

Wedding Memories &
Photographs

Wedding Memories & Photographs

Wedding Memories & Photographs

Wedding Memories & Photographs

Wedding Memories & Photographs

Wedding Memories & Photographs

Wedding Memories &
Photographs

Wedding Memories & Photographs

Wedding Memories & Photographs

Wedding Memories & Photographs

Wedding Memories &
Photographs